Q&A Kids

THE WATER CYCLE

AMY CHAPMAN ANGELIKA SCUDAMORE

WINDMILL BOOKS

Published in 2026 by Windmill Books,
an Imprint of Rosen Publishing
2544 Clinton St.
Buffalo, NY 14224

First published in Great Britain in 2026
by Wayland

Editor: Sarah Peutrill
Designer: Lisa Peacock

Some of the text in this book was first
published in Fact Cat: The Water Cycle
by Izzi Howell

Cataloging-in-Publication Data
Names: Chapman, Amy, author. | Scudamore, Angelika, illustrator.
Title: The water cycle / Amy Chapman, illustrated by Angelika Scudamore.
Description: Buffalo, NY : Windmill Books, 2026. | Series: Q & A kids | Includes glossary and index.
Identifiers: ISBN 9781725396371 (pbk.) | ISBN 9781725396388 (library bound) | ISBN 9781725396395 (ebook)
Subjects: LCSH: Hydrologic cycle--Juvenile literature.
Classification: LCC GB848.C437 2026 | DDC 551.48--dc23

Printed in the United States of America

CPSIA Compliance Information: Batch #CSWM26
For Further Information contact Rosen Publishing
at 1-800-237-9932

Find us on

CONTENTS

Water	4
Living Things and Water	6
Solids, Liquids, and Gases	8
The Water Cycle	10
Evaporation	12
Condensation	14
Clouds and Rain	16
Snow, Sleet, and Hail	18
Underground Water	20
Rivers	22
Oceans and Seas	24
Controlling Water	26
Saving Water	28
Quiz	30
Glossary	31
Index and Some Answers	32

Can you spot the water drops in this book? There are 14 to find, not counting me.

WATER

Q. What is water?

A. Water is a clear liquid that has no color, taste, or smell. It falls from clouds as rain and is used for drinking and washing.

Water is very important for living things. Animals and plants need water to survive.

Most of the Earth's surface is covered in water. Nearly all of this water is salt water, found in seas and oceans. A small amount of it is fresh water.

THINK ABOUT IT

The water in
rivers is fresh water.
Where else can you
find fresh water?

LIVING THINGS AND WATER

Q. Do all living things need water?

A. Yes, all plants and animals need water to survive.

Most animals drink fresh water. Animals such as these ducks drink fresh water from ponds and rivers.

People need to drink plenty of water each day. We drink fresh water from bottles, or water that comes from taps in our homes.

Plants use their roots to take in water from the soil.

FIND IT

Find four sources of water for people and animals to drink from in the picture.

SOLIDS, LIQUIDS, AND GASES

Q. Why are ice cubes hard?

A. Ice cubes are water that has turned into a solid. Solid water is hard.

Water can have three states: solid, liquid, or gas. The state of water depends on its temperature.

When water freezes, it becomes a solid. The iceberg is made of ice.

When ice is heated, it melts into liquid water. As a liquid, water can flow into the shape of any container you put it in.

When water reaches boiling point, it becomes a gas, called water vapor, which can move through the air.

FIND OUT

Water freezes at 32 degrees Fahrenheit (0°C). At what temperature does water boil?

Icebergs are made of frozen water.

THE WATER CYCLE

Q. Can we make more water on Earth?

A. No, we cannot. No water is made or lost in the water cycle. The amount of water on Earth is the same water that was around during the time of the dinosaurs!

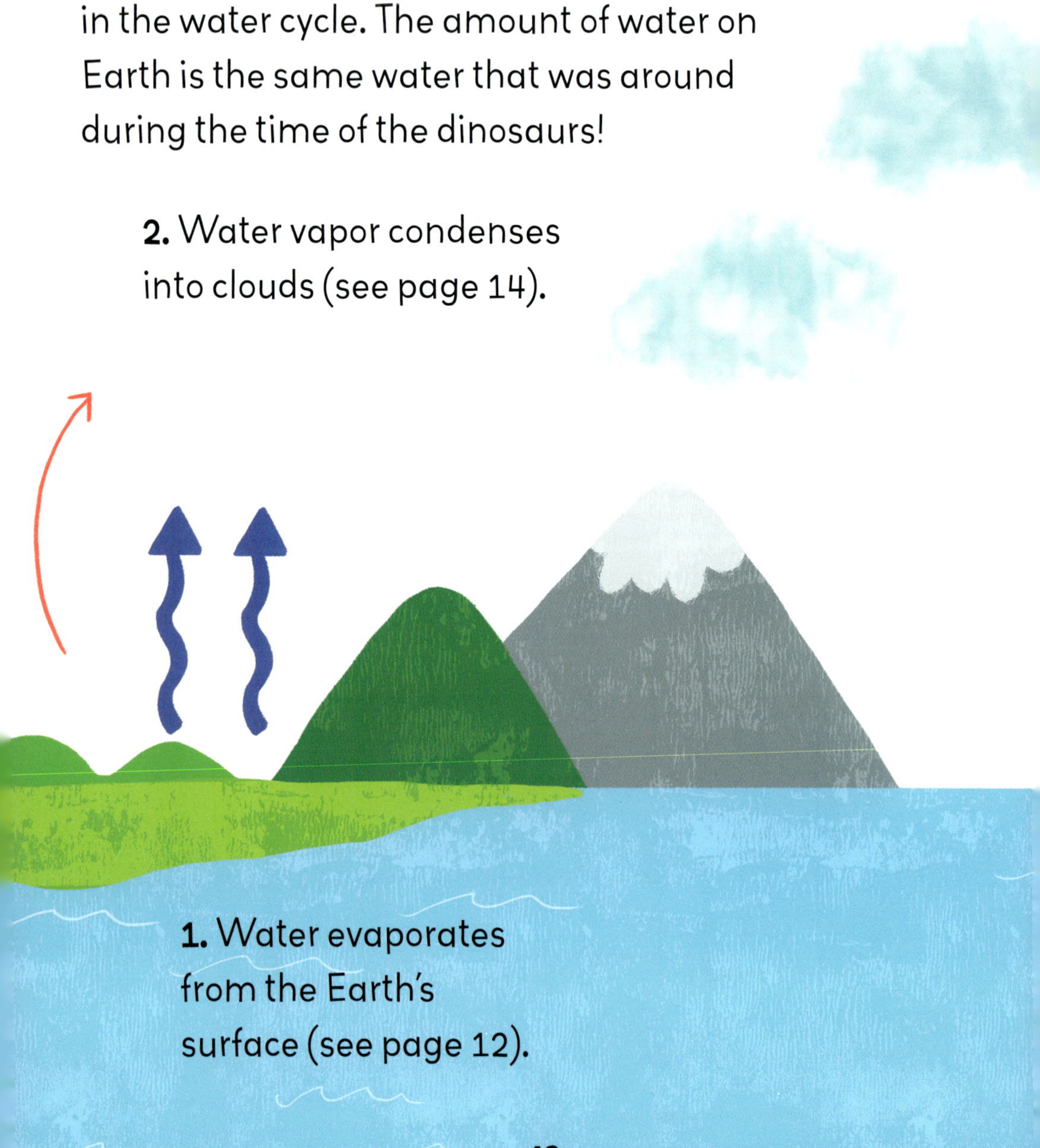

Water is always moving from the surface of Earth to the atmosphere and back again. This movement is called the water cycle.

EVAPORATION

Q. When a puddle dries up, is the water lost?

A. No, the water has evaporated and turned into water vapor, which moves through the air.

At the beginning of the water cycle, heat from the Sun warms up water on the Earth's surface. When liquid water is heated, it evaporates and turns into water vapor.

Water evaporates from the surface of lakes, rivers, and puddles.

Sometimes you can see evaporation taking place. If it rains on a hot day, the puddles of water on the pavement quickly disappear. This is because the liquid water has evaporated into water vapor.

THINK ABOUT IT

Wet laundry dries when water evaporates from it. Why do clothes dry faster when they are hung outside on a sunny warm day?

CONDENSATION

Q. How are clouds made?

A. As water vapor is a gas, it rises up into the atmosphere. It is colder in the sky than on the ground. As the water vapor cools, it turns into clouds. This is called condensation.

We sometimes see condensation on a glass of cold water. The water vapor in the air cools down when it hits the cold glass. This creates small drops of water on the glass.

THINK ABOUT IT

Why might you see condensation on a window?

SNOW, SLEET, AND HAIL

Q. What is snow?

A. Snowflakes are made of tiny ice crystals stuck together.

When the weather is really cold, rain freezes. It falls to the ground as snow or hail.

Usually snowflakes melt by the time they reach the ground, but if the air is cold enough, they fall as snow.

Sleet is halfway between rain and snow.

Hail drops are pieces of ice that fall from clouds.

FIND IT

All snowflakes have six sides or points, but no two snowflakes are the same! This picture has two the same by mistake. Can you find the matching pair?

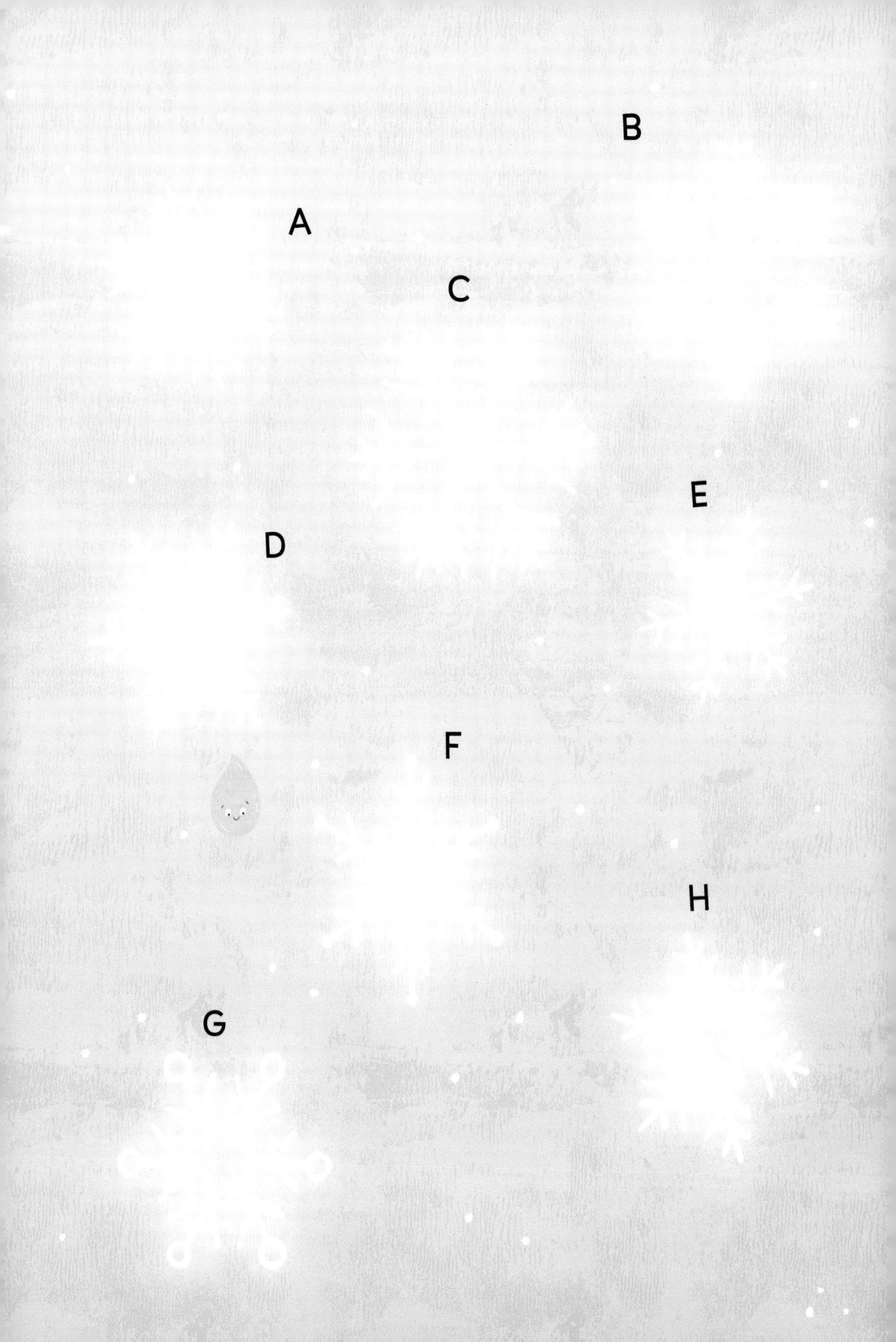
A
B
C
D
E
F
G
H

UNDERGROUND WATER

Q. Does rain just make puddles?

A. Rain that lands on a hard surface like pavement will make a puddle. But when rainwater reaches soil, much of it soaks into the Earth's surface.

Plant roots take in some of the water, but most of it travels deep underground. When rainwater moves through holes in the ground, it makes underground lakes.

Sometimes, underground water flows back above ground to form a spring. Springs are often the sources of rivers.

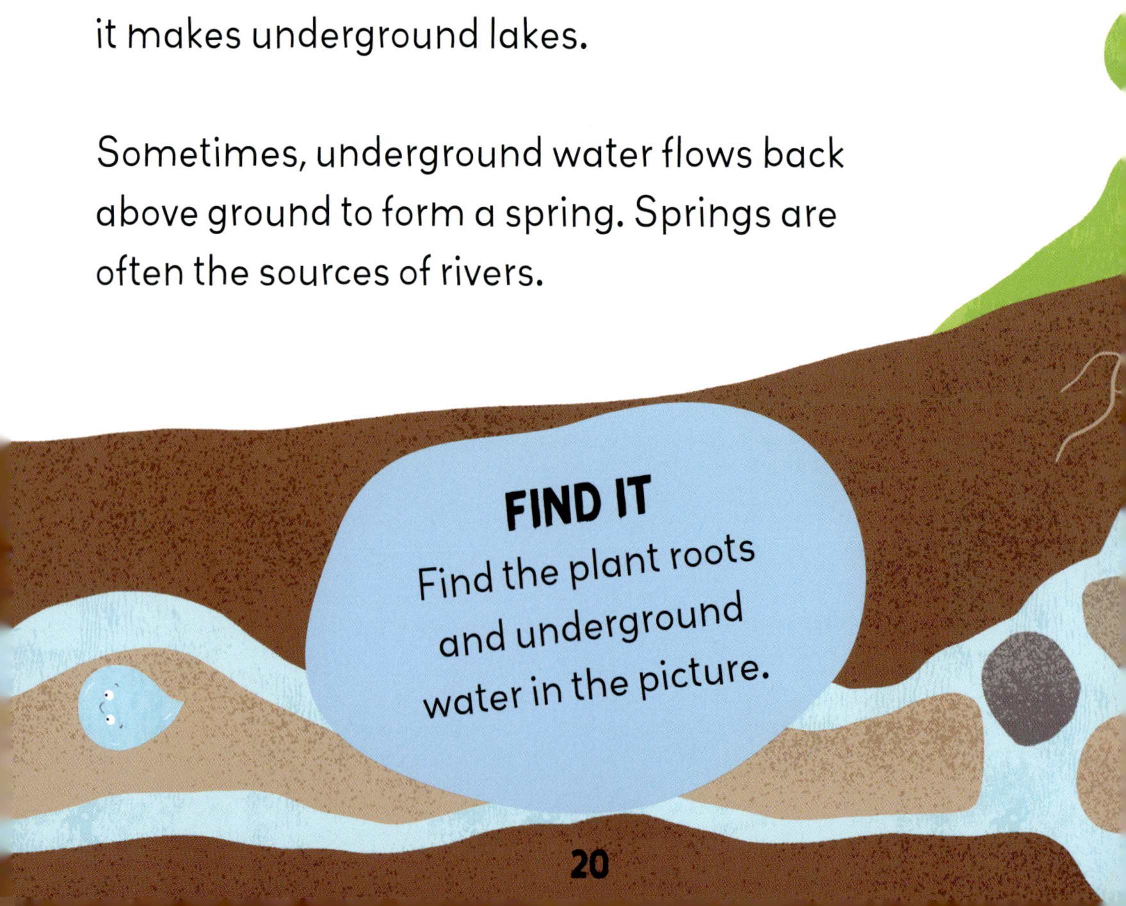

FIND IT

Find the plant roots and underground water in the picture.

RIVERS

Q. Does all river water come from rain?

A. No, most does not. A small amount of the water that falls as rain enters rivers.

Rivers start life as small streams. The source of the water may be a spring on a hillside, the meltwater from a glacier, or melting snow. The water in a stream flows quickly, tumbling over rocks and wearing them away.

As more water enters a stream, it becomes larger and it becomes known as a river.

Some of the water that falls as rain runs across the surface of the Earth. It flows downhill until it reaches a stream or river.

Rivers get wider as more water flows into them.

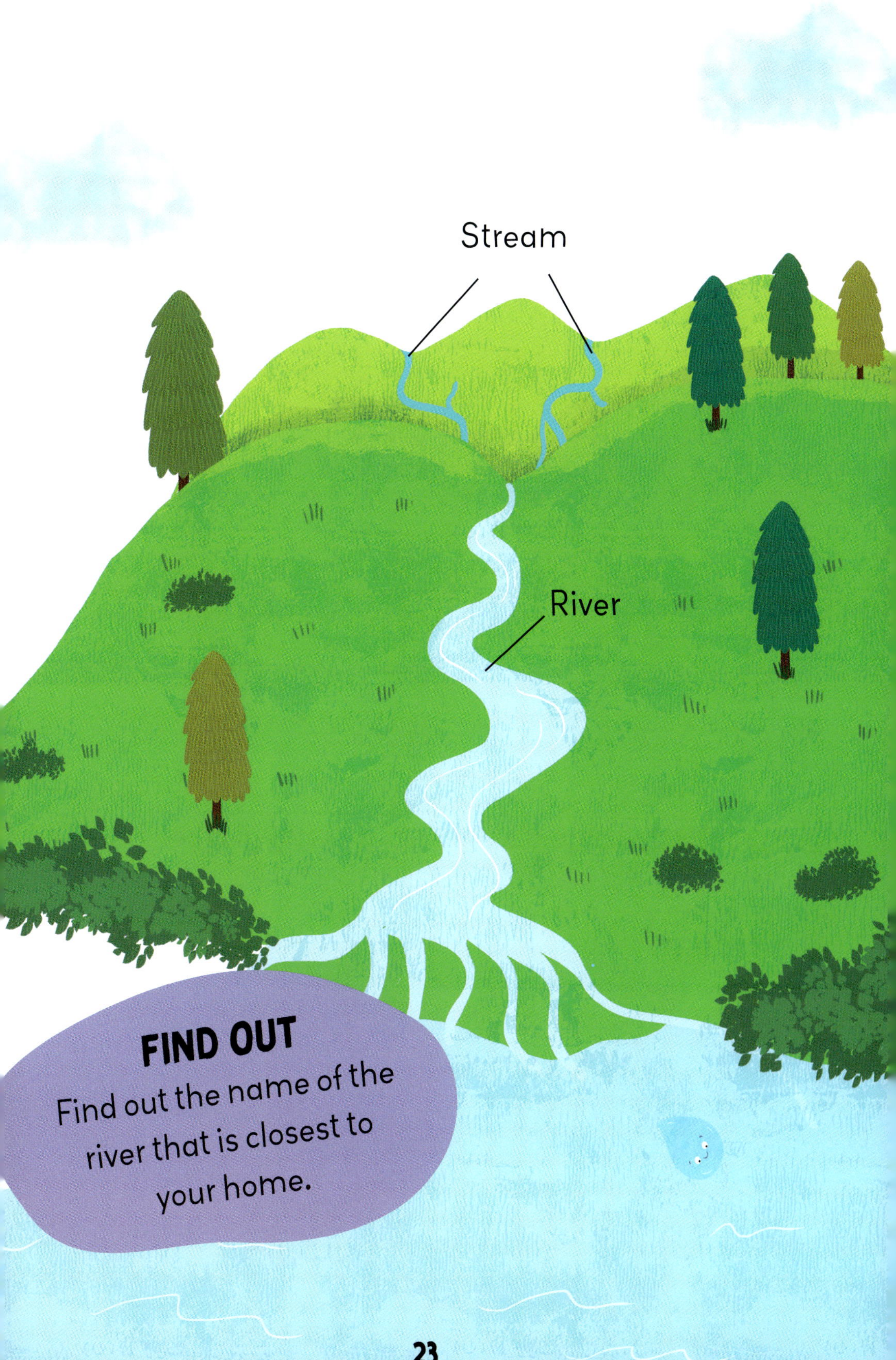

FIND OUT

Find out the name of the river that is closest to your home.

OCEANS AND SEAS

Q. Where is the river water going?

A. All rivers flow into the sea.

The place where a river meets the sea is called an estuary. The water in an estuary is a mixture of salt water and fresh water.

The sea is salty water. People and other animals that live on land cannot drink salt water because our bodies, especially our kidneys, cannot deal with the salt. We rely on fresh water.

The water that reaches the sea will evaporate into water vapor and the water cycle will start again.

FIND IT

Isla has made a scrapbook of an ocean scene. Which creatures don't belong and don't like salt water?

A.
B.
C.
D.
E.
F.
G.
I.
H.
K.
J.
L.

CONTROLLING WATER

Q. How does water come out of the tap?

A. Pipes bring clean water into our homes for cooking, drinking, and washing.

Controlling water makes it easier for us to use. Humans can control the flow of water.

We also build large strong walls, called dams, to control how much water flows down a river. Dams stop rivers from flooding after lots of rain.

FIND IT

The picture shows parts of another water cycle – how water is treated. In this example, where does the water go after sewage treatment?

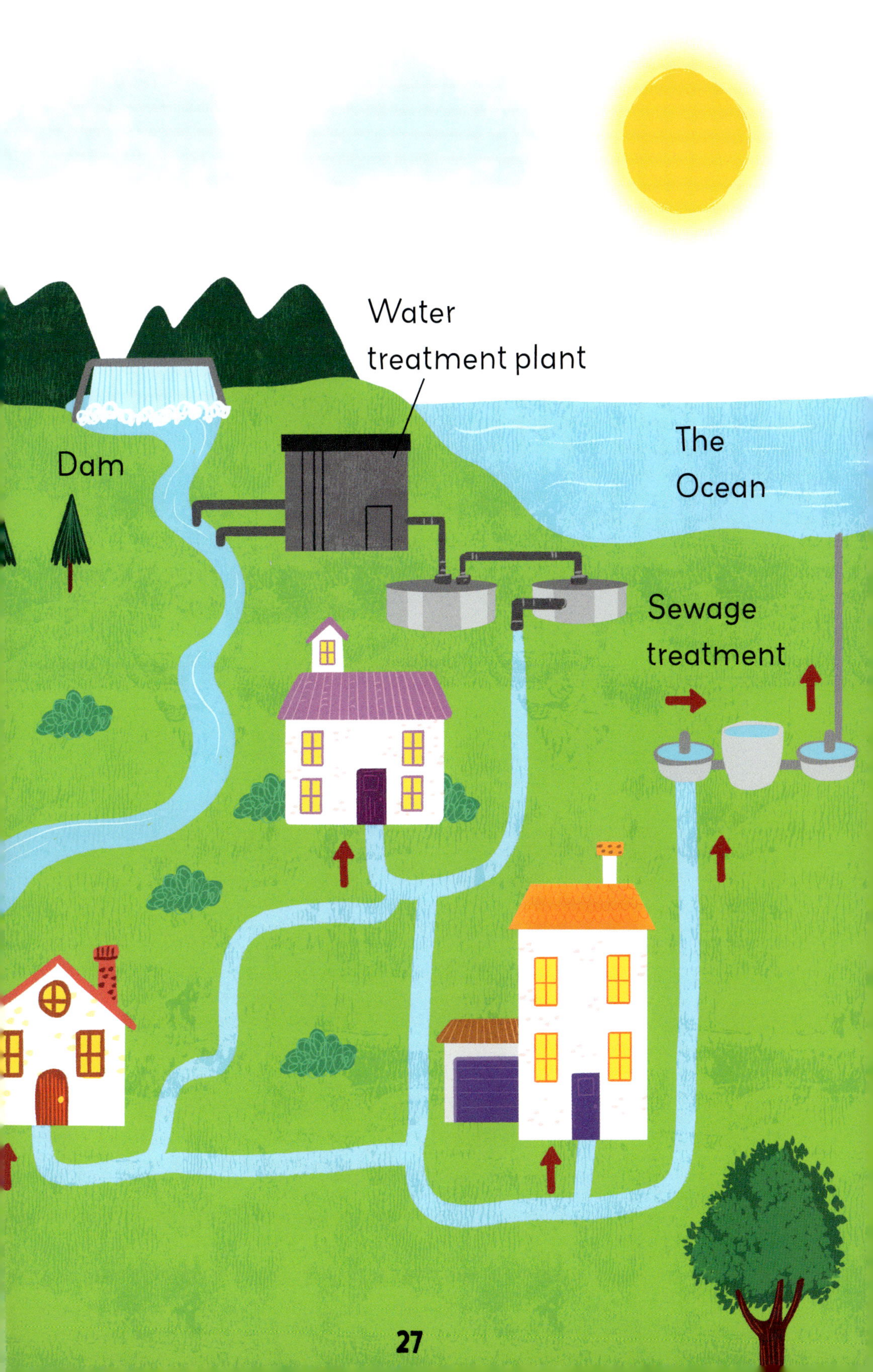
Water
treatment plant
Dam
The
Ocean
Sewage
treatment

SAVING WATER

Q. If there's always the same amount of water on Earth, why should we try to save water?

A. As there are more people in the world, we need to farm more crops and make more things in factories. This will lead to more water usage. However, there is only a limited amount of water, so savings have to be made to keep us from running out of water.

THINK ABOUT IT

There are many ways to reduce our use of water. You can make a difference too! Look at the pictures and work out how the children are saving water. What other ways can you think of?

A.

B.

C.

QUIZ

1. Most water on Earth is salt water. True or not true?

a) true

b) not true

2. Which state is ice?

a) solid

b) liquid

c) gas

3. Water evaporates when it cools down. True or not true?

a) true

b) not true

4. What is condensation?

a) when ice warms up and melts into liquid water

b) when liquid water cools down and turns into ice

c) when water vapor cools down and turns into liquid water

5. The source of a river is where it starts. True or not true?

a) true

b) not true

Quiz answers

1. a – true
2. a – solid
3. b – not true – it evaporates when it heats up
4. c – when water vapor cools down and turns into liquid water
5. a – true

GLOSSARY

atmosphere the air around Earth

boiling point the temperature that a liquid boils at

condense to change from a gas to a liquid as it gets colder

dam a strong wall built across a river to control how much water passes through

estuary the place where a river flows into the sea

evaporate to change from a liquid to a gas as it gets warmer

flooding when a lot of water covers an area that is usually dry, often because a river has too much water in it

freeze when a liquid turns hard and solid because of the cold

fresh water water without salt in it, found in lakes and rivers

gas something that is neither a solid nor a liquid, such as air

liquid something that is neither a solid nor a gas, such as milk

living things something that is alive, such as a plant or an animal

melt to turn from a solid to a liquid as it gets warmer

salt water water with salt in it, found in seas and oceans

sewage dirty water which flows out of homes and factories in waste pipes

solid something that is neither a liquid nor a gas, such as a table

source the starting point of a river

spring a place where underground water flows out of the ground

state the state of an object can be solid, liquid, or gas

surface the top part of something

survive to stay alive

temperature how hot or cold something is

treatment the process of cleaning water

water vapor water as a gas

INDEX

animals 4, 6, 10, 24–25

condensation 10, 14–15

dams 26

evaporation 10, 12–13, 24

fresh water 4–7, 24, 26

hail 18

ice 8–9, 18

oceans 4, 24

plants 4, 6, 20

rain 4, 16, 18, 20, 22, 26

rivers 5, 6, 13, 20, 24, 26

salt water 4, 24

seas 4, 11, 24

sleet 18

snow 18, 22

water treatment plant 27

water vapor 8, 10, 12–14, 16, 24

SOME ANSWERS

p.5 Fresh water is also found in ponds, lakes, and streams and frozen in ice

p. 6 water fountain; drinking bottle; lake; puddle

p. 9 212°F (100°C)

p. 13 Water evaporates faster in warmer temperatures

p. 14 Glass might be colder than air so the water in the air cools and condenses on the window

p. 16 1A; 2E; 3C; 4F; 5D; 6B

p. 18 D and H

p. 24 E, F, K (mice, cats, and frogs don't live in salt water)

p. 26 the ocean

p.28 A – using a shower instead of a bath; B – turning off the tap while brushing teeth; C – using rain water from a rain barrel